A Mermaid Like Me

Also By Aerwyna

Beach

A Mermaid Like Me

A Collection Of Mermaid Poetry

Aerwyna

To my mermaid, Christmas 2019, who swims in my heart! Merry Christmas! Love, Mike

Copyright © 2019 Aerwyna. All rights reserved.

https://www.UniquelyMermaid.com/contact-form.html

Aerwyna@UniquelyMermaid.com

First Edition

This work is an expression of the author's creativity. Names, characters, businesses, places, events and incidents are either the products of the author's imagination or used in a fictitious manner. Any resemblance to actual persons, living or dead, or actual events is purely coincidental.

ISBN: 978-1-087-09714-5

Cover design by OliviaProDesign

https://www.fiverr.com/oliviaprodesign

Cover photo by Katalinks

https://depositphotos.com/portfolio-1023099.html

Silhouette images by Gluiki

https://www.shutterstock.com/g/Gluiki

For The Mermaid Inside Of You

Contents

Part I – In The Current — 1

    Emerging — 3
    If I Were A Mermaid — 4
    Metamorphosis — 6
    Halfway — 7
    The Mermaid Inside — 8
    Surfacing — 9
    The Endless Sea — 10
    The Dreamer — 11
    I Am A Mermaid — 12
    A Mermaid Like Me — 14

Part II – The Seven Seas — 17

    Salty Maidens — 19
    Ask A Mermaid — 20
    The Pirates & The Mermaids — 24

Part III – Drifting — 27

    Sirenic Voices — 29
    In A Mermaid's Dream — 30
    Brushstrokes — 31
    The Sea Garden — 32
    In The Shallows — 34
    A Mermaid Christmas — 37
    Through A Mermaid's Eyes — 38
    Sea Lights — 40

Part IV – The Depths	*43*
Aruba Descending	45
Before The Wind	52
Part V – Uncharted Waters	*59*
Do You Know Me?	61
About The Author	63

Like A Mermaid In The Sea, I Am Free To Be Uniquely Me

Part I – *In The Current*

To paraphrase the dictionary definition of current, *water moving in a specific direction within a surrounding body of water moving at a slower speed*, is most appropriate for the poems in this chapter. In order to be your unique self, you must draw from within and become the current that constantly forges through regardless of the movement around you.

Emerging

Under the sea I am free
Caressed by a wave I am brave
Among the coral I am immortal
Beneath the surface is what I crave

Dare I do more than flip my tail
If I leave the water I might fail
Cautiously swimming toward the sun
I break the surface for a trial run

It's okay to be me and live here, too
The sea is beautiful from either view
Above the surface others will see
That beneath the surface I am still me

If I Were A Mermaid

If I were a mermaid I would know within me
Lies a power and a force as big as the sea
I would dive where the bottom is smooth and clear
Knowing that I'd find safety here
If I lose my way I would follow the tides
And change course until confusion subsides

If I were a mermaid I would know what to do
Life's frustrations would not throw me askew
Turbulent currents would not alter my plans
My track I would follow through shifting sands
I'd stick to my purpose and reach my goals
As easily as swimming onto shallow shoals

If I were a mermaid I would like myself
And dust off the dreams that I've stored on a shelf
Others' opinions would no longer build like a dam
Holding me back from doing all that I can
I would burst forth like a river in pursuit of the sea
And become the best version of who I want to be

If I were a mermaid I would hold the key
To unlock the treasures buried deep within me

Metamorphosis

What steps can I take of my own creation
To begin my beautiful mermaid transformation
As I look in the mirror it reflects back to me
How I can become a siren of the sea

A few adjustments here and there
Let's start with long, flowing hair
Upon which a crown of shells I'll place
And sparkling glitter applied to my face

Mixed shades of shadow lining my eyes
Upon my gaze one becomes mesmerized
I slip into my tail and turn to see
A mermaid in the mirror staring back at me!

Halfway

I saw a mermaid at the beach
She seemed so near, just within my reach
The closer I moved she was much farther still
Am I dreaming this scene against my will?

For I would not frighten a mermaid away
No, instead her fears I would allay
So we could meet halfway just as the sea touches the sky
And form new horizons as each day goes by

The Mermaid Inside

There's magic in wearing mermaid tails
Flying through water as if I had scales
Keeping pace with dolphins and whales
In weightless rhythm my body sails

In sun-dappled water my tail shimmers
Each scale a jewel through which light glimmers
With a spin of my fin I swiftly dash
Diving below as I make a big splash

Propelled under water I'm filled with glee
Buoyant and jubilant, ever so free
Arms gently floating while I glide
On the outside I've become the mermaid inside

Surfacing

I am different
I am unique
It is not approval that I seek
Just freedom and expression
Of the me deep inside
A surfacing from within
A force I cannot hide

The Endless Sea

At times I'm fearful and want to hide from the world
Rolled into safekeeping like a sail furled
A port in the storm where I can take refuge
A hidden cove protected from life's deluge

Is there such a place where I can be free
Swept away from worry, care and anxiety
In all of its vastness I turn to the sea
As wave upon wave washes over me

Like a mermaid I'd swim away from shore
Until I could not see land anymore
And stream through the depths where I will break free
As free as a mermaid in the endless sea

The Dreamer

A beautiful mermaid visited me
I knew at once she came from the sea
To show me a path and direction to take
A spell to awaken a journey I must make

I now see so clearly what was hidden in me
For I am a dreamer and it's okay to be
A dream like a wave that moves with the tide
Closer and faster to the shore it rides

Unfolding and spreading upon the beach
Saturating each grain of sand within reach
As does a dream when released from inside
Like a message in a bottle traveling far and wide

I Am A Mermaid

I am a mermaid through and through
With seaweed in my hair and no need for shoes
That would explain my craving for salt
And first place in swimming as if by default

My penchant for weaving shells through my hair
Has caused passersby to stop and stare
As I make my way home from a long day at school
Where the first thing I'll do is jump in the pool

When my friends and I go to the beach
I can't sit and chat when the sea is in reach
Lifeguards are amazed at how far I can go
Without being caught in the undertow

My closet is filled with tops made of shells
And rows of mermaid tails in colorful pastels
Inside of my desk kept under lock and key
A book of mermaid spells that I practice on me

My room is illuminated with soft underwater lights
As sounds of the deep serenade me through the night
I sleep on a waterbed and dream among the waves
Of life inside my very own sea cave

I am a mermaid as I'm sure you can see
That pretending weaves magic and causes it to be
So if you would like to be a mermaid, too
Start spinning your tale and watch it come true!

A Mermaid Like Me

Where is the mermaid who is just like me?
Is she beautiful and fragile with a touch of whimsy?
If I find her I'll ask her how I can be
Just like a mermaid, a mermaid like me

My hair would be long with waves and curls
My body adorned with shells and pearls
I'd move like a dancer, my stage the sea
And be just like a mermaid, a mermaid like me

I would sit at the very edge of the beach
So the water was just within my reach
A safe place to escape to, the tranquil sea
Where I'd be just like a mermaid, a mermaid like me

No one would ever bother me here
I could swim where I want to without any fear
Away from expectations I am truly free
Just like a mermaid, a mermaid like me

Free me from "shoulds" and habits of old
A powerful tail would make me feel bold
Then I could fly away free in the sea
And be just like a mermaid, a mermaid like me

Part II – *The Seven Seas*

Whether it's seafaring stories, legends of the deep, swashbuckling tales, or sunken treasure, life is a never-ending adventure on the Seven Seas!

Salty Maidens

Salty maidens come hither with your wine
And bring me a cask of your finest brine
Upon which I'll steer me ship and me sails
The Seven Seas I'll navigate with me bow at your tails

'Tis a mighty ship of fools that refuses to see
A maiden of the deep surrounding thee
Long guiding mariners while submerged in stealth
To a captain she is the sea herself

Ask A Mermaid

I would like to ask a mermaid who lives in the sea
Please explain why you haven't shown yourself to me...

I will take it upon myself to speak for all of us
We don't know why everyone is in such a fuss
It's easy to see us, you just have to believe
Because reality is created by what you perceive

By the way, mermaids, where do you live?
Do you have homes of your own, is there a hint you can give?

The sea is our home where some love to roam
Using currents and tides we swim to new zones
While others stay close to family and friends
And some choose to visit every now and again

Tell me, mermaids, are you alone?
Are there mermen and merfolk that you have known?

Of course there are mermen and merfolk, too
Don't forget merchildren, as was I before I grew

Mermaids aren't real, they're just fairy tales
How can you possibly be a human with scales?

We have adapted to live in the sea
Compared to those on land we are more free
We have evolved from where you are
We've stretched our imaginations to get this far
Your mention of fairy is true, you see
For we are elemental spirits, as we've come to be
Fairies of air, water, fire and earth
We are what gives nature its birth

*So what do you do with yourselves every day
Just swim and sunbathe, comb your hair and play?*

Ah, you amuse me with questions such as these
For life is very busy here in the Seven Seas
When you call to us for help we are quick to respond
Wherever waters are turbulent and need to be calmed
As water spirits we move the seas in accordance with nature's plan
Which you direct and guide, although most don't know they can

*What do mermaids eat?
You probably go for salty fare, but what about something sweet?*

A fine wine for us is brine
It has all we need to keep us feeling fine
Above the surface we like to snack on things within our reach
Wild berries of every sort that grow quite near the beach

I would like to ask a mermaid, how do you sleep?
Is it possible to take a snooze in the fathoms of the deep?

Like you, mermaids need downtime to unwind and to rest
A relaxed state of being that keeps us at our best
Most just float in a tranquil state, a daydream so to speak
Eyes closed and dreaming, counting fish instead of sheep
Some will lie upon the sand of a beach late at night
A restful pose with sounds of surf beneath a soft moonlight

But what about…

Thousands of questions remain unanswered, but to me that is okay
For belief speaks louder than words, causing your perceptions to sway
Then you will not have to question me because you'll have no doubt
That mermaids are as real as you and that's what this is about!

The Pirates & The Mermaids

"Cap'n, Cap'n, there is a lass, says I
She has a tail, I've seen her swim by!"
"Blimey, sailor, it's all the grog ye drank
Back ye go up the crow's nest or ye walk the plank!

"A fool this lad, he's lost his head
Many a day at sea can bring on the dread
It's worth it all, mind ye, for the booty we take
A-plunderin' and a-pillagin' for our pockets' sake

"For we are pirates of the Seven Seas
Sailin' the oceans and doin' as we please
Linin' our pockets and fillin' our crates
With gold doubloons and silver pieces of eight"

"Cap'n, Cap'n, storm's a-brewin'
Sails a-billowin', we're headed for ruin!"
"Batten down the hatches, lad, and secure me precious loot
For a storm has never scuttled this ship and of that I'm absolute"

"Shiver me timbers, Cap'n, the coffers slipped into the drink!"
"Avast ye, sailor, hook those crates before me booty sinks!"
"It's the lass with the tail, Cap'n, swimmin' towards the crates
And all around her many tails, blimey, she's brought her mates!"

"Good day to ye, sirs, we are mermaids of the Seven Seas
And just like ye we roam the waters doing as we please
It pleases us greatly to take these coins of gold and silver hue
And return them to their rightful owners, and this we shall certainly do"

And so the legend can be traced back to that very day
When mermaids took the pirates' loot and hauled it all away
Where it landed no one knows for it was never seen again
But since that time a pirate fears when one mermaid turns into ten!

Part III – *Drifting*

At times it's best to step back and observe, be a witness to the flow of life around you. One can drift without participating, and allow stillness to penetrate the senses.

Sirenic Voices

I hear mermaids singing to me
Sirenic voices from the sapphire sea
A fluid chorus of ethereal sounds
Flowing as waves upon the sand they pound

These are not the songs that once sunk ships
Harmony, not treachery, passes through their lips
Melodies on the wind that ebb and recede
Like a delicate wind chime of sea glass and bead

In A Mermaid's Dream

And so I slumber in a mermaid's dream
As floating shadows through water stream
A seahorse appears in front of me at will
Meeting my gaze like a statue so still

Sea anemones waving tentacles at me
Forgetting how painful their sting can be
Clouds of jellyfish in a celestial dance
Must I awaken from this aquatic trance?

For here I am a mermaid, scales and all
Breathing underwater I now recall
I can live in both worlds above and below the sea
For anything is possible with a dream inside of me

Brushtrokes

Oft depicted in mermaid art
Graceful, flowing, worlds apart
A classic beauty both strong and frail
Silken mane entwining body and tail

Beautiful siren of the seas
Awash in color, an artist's tease
Circular strokes in perpetual motion
On canvas she's born a goddess of the ocean

The Sea Garden

Through stalks of kelp a forest I see
Living and breathing beneath the sea
Shafts of sunlight shining through
Turn moss green leaves into a golden hue
I weave my way through these giant plants
As leaves brush my skin in their aquatic dance

Floating over an underwater lea
Seagrass set in motion by the movement of the sea
I pause to loll on its soft green bed
Out of the corner of my eye I glimpse something red

Shades of ruby, crimson, scarlet and rose
Found where the bloom of red algae grows
Sprays of lavender, violet, mauve and amethyst
As purple sea urchins to and fro twist

A pallet of color so brilliantly infused
On a reef of coral in rainbow hues
While fish of every shape and size
Add splashes of iridescence before my eyes

A sensual oasis to unwind and release
As I drift languidly over this sea garden masterpiece

In The Shallows

In the shallows I linger, treading water
Here in the wings I'm ocean's daughter
Lifting my eyes just above the surface
I spy like a periscope from the abyss

As life's theater is staged before my eyes
Scenes unrehearsed, lines improvised
Many vignettes unfold before my sight
All played out under the afternoon light

A couple on the beach walking hand in hand
Barefoot and laughing on the warm moist sand
Each meeting of their eyes begins a new phase
A momentum building further into love's daze

And there is a woman up on the hill
With a basket of clothes she endlessly fills
Up on the line with sheets to the wind
Unclipped and down again, neatly folded and trimmed

Over on the rocks sits a wistful lass
A melancholy stance with eyes downcast
The cause of her dismay remains unknown
Reflected in the water as she sits there alone

A castle is built on the beach by hand
Turrets and moats of water and sand
This fortress formed by shovel and pail
Is a kingdom overthrown as waves prevail

On the jetty sits a man with easel and paint
Capturing the scene uphill, so quaint
To him she is a study of strength and repose
To her it's just another day of folding clothes

Dangling from the pier is a line with a hook
Here in the shallows a scene I mistook
For a fisherman's catch is not what I wish to be
Exit stage left, it's the deep sea for me!

A Mermaid Christmas

A mermaid Christmas is a wonder to behold
Stash away your chimney stockings, if I may be so bold
Over the fireplace instead will hang a row of mermaid tails
I wonder what surprises hide inside these colorful scales

A Christmas tree adorned with shells all sparkling and aglitter
Reflecting light around the room as floating candles flicker
While snow globes filled with ocean scenes delight each passerby
A mermaid hides within the glass from which she then can spy

And glimpse the happiness of the occasion with faces all aglow
Just like the warmth of the ocean as it melts each flake of snow
Only to be stirred up again with each passing year
As the season of glad tidings and good cheer draws near

Through A Mermaid's Eyes

As clouds burst forth upon the sea
Below the surface a mermaid sees
Delicate raindrops that pitter and patter
Forming circular patterns that swiftly scatter

While heavy downpours create clouds of bubbles
An effervescence of beads that perpetually doubles
Mighty winds stir up waves that crash below
A maelstrom of water disrupting current and flow

Lingering momentarily in the sea foam bath
A powerful twist of the tail changes her path
Blades of seagrass dance to and fro
Parting and swaying as she dives below

Schools of fish dart before her eyes
Spotted and striped and some in disguise
Every color of the rainbow in a wavelike dance
While a few meet her gaze with a sideways glance

In the distance she spies a Spanish galleon
Its cargo once heavy with gemstones and medallions
Long ago salvaged for its sunken treasure
Riches beyond what one can measure

She turns her gaze up to the surface
A cacophony of noise, a disruptive circus
To a mermaid the idea seems so remote
That humans need engines in order to float!

Sea Lights

Somewhere in the depths of the ocean at night
Shine clouds and waves of brilliant light
A mermaid's fireworks inside the sea
Bioluminescence as it's known to be

Jellyfish illuminating like lava lamps
A slow ascent their undulating dance
Become lanterns along a mermaid's course
Shadowed at times by a crossing seahorse

Glowworms light the sea like a million twinkling stars
A mermaid's fairy lights from their gleaming repertoires
Strung together like melee diamonds, far too many to count
A night sky lit by fireflies or meteor showers tantamount

Flashlight fish blink their eyes and emit a flickering light
Like floating candles tossed about on a windy night
Like a galaxy of planets and stars on a backdrop of dark skies
These dazzling displays of light are reflected in a mermaid's eyes

Part IV – *The Depths*

Hopelessness, sadness, grief, emptiness – to experience the depths of emotion is not for the faint of heart. At times we are all artists painting self-portraits from this palette of dark colors.

Aruba Descending

Aruba descending, descending down
Into subsurface currents previously unfound
Spinning and twisting against her will
Tail splaying helplessly in this malevolent swirl

Harsh is the weather above and below
Flotsam and jetsam hurling to and fro
Where it's dark and it's cold with no air to breathe
Yet here she remains afraid to leave

Named for an island near a reef where she was found
Where at a young age she became dispiritedly bound
To the rules of those from whom she sought approval
A debris so entrenched with no hope for removal

Presiding over a collection in her sea cave
Skeletons from the past, a watery grave
A skull named Anger dominates this place
It's written all over what once was her face
Wrist bones show grooves where razors cut deep
Releasing lifeblood's hold, a permanent sleep

Buried inside a shell of her own making
Barnacle-encrusted, salt and seaweed caking
A cold, clammy feeling upon her is leached
Creating a tomb which cannot be breached

"I carry my own anchors and chains
As a series of shipwrecks scourge through my veins
Pierced by the splinters of decaying wood
Drops of blood are my offering, a way to make good
On promises I repeatedly broke to myself
Dreams I've left lying on a dusty old shelf

"A shiny object had me lured and hooked
Signaling danger which I overlooked
Helplessly falling into a tattered net
Trapped and entangled in this fate I've beget

"My dreams were like gemstones of dazzling hues
Sparkling and brilliant, too precious to lose
Snatched by the pirates of deception and self-pity
Their swords raised in triumph, faces hardened and gritty"

Aruba descending upon her throne
A kingdom within to her unknown
Pearls of wisdom she has yet to string
A muted voice that longs to sing

Garbage from the surface litters her mind
Swill and debris floating in kind
Poisons and pollutants leak from barrels
Tossed without thought to whom it imperils

"I am like a sea sponge soaked with emotion
Saturated and drenched, seeping into the ocean
A fragile encasement of water and air
With holes so many, too easily I tear

"I am raw and naked, scars exposed as I float
Peered at from above through a glass-bottomed boat
My foundation is weak like a castle made of sand
Precariously perched between ocean and land

"I claw and clench my way across the seafloor
I feed from the bottom, too scared to do more
Grasping for a morsel to satiate my taste
Swallowed by fear, life's most toxic waste"

Aruba descending into the comfort of sleep
Relieved of the watch she so vigilantly keeps
Her dreams are a muddle of thoughts unexpressed
Like the rising of the tide, seldom at rest

Aruba defending an awkward position
Made worse by her skilled art of indecision
"I am slippery like the eel
I don't trust myself or how I feel
All of my vain attempts to step away from the ledge
Have only pushed me further toward the edge"

Aruba descending into the depths of madness
Stoic, emotionless, neither gladness nor sadness
What is madness anyway but something misunderstood
A jab at mediocrity and acting as you should

Aruba descending into the bottomless sea
Come out of your tailspin and set yourself free
Ascend like a diver, decompressing as you go
Painlessly rising from the darkness below

Aruba ascending from the depths of the ocean
Releasing a lifetime of buried emotion
Narrowly teetering on an even keel
Breaking the surface, it's time to heal

Before The Wind

Upon a rock I sit close to shore
Staring out to sea forevermore
For I once loved a captain of a ship
My heart he held within his grip

Many years ago was this tale of the sea
Bringing up so many emotions dormant in me
We were like two ships that pass in the night
A fleeting moment that burned so bright

So handsome was he by the cut of his jib
With a clever sense of humor he'd completely ad lib
And now I find myself all at sea
With this sad remembrance of what wasn't to be

We may have been rocking the boat in our quest for love
A mermaid and a captain are not what most would think of
Perhaps they'll come around to see that love is there
Between two whose hearts are entwined in all they share

I first saw him off of England's Cornish coast
As I surreptitiously swam around his boat
A fine clipper ship over two hundred feet in length
I would watch him from afar, admiring his strength

The year was 1891
A cargo of spices his ship would run
I watched its comings and goings from Falmouth port
The merchant trade in those days a prosperous sort

One day as they were headed back out to sea
I saw him peering at what I thought was me
His spyglass pointed in my direction
Perhaps it was just a mistaken reflection

Months would pass before his return
Until one day I spotted "Lorelei" on the stern
Ironically named for the siren whose voice would sink ships
A fate he and his crew would certainly eclipse

The clipper's great sails cast a shadow over the starboard side
So there among the lapping waves I would hide
As I watched him walking briskly along the decks
The command of his stance kept the crew in check

Suddenly he turned and looked directly at me
I was close enough that he didn't need a spyglass to see
When our eyes met and locked it was as if I knew him
Call it intuition, just a hunch, or maybe a whim
Something stirred inside of me
As I drifted so calmly in the gray-blue sea

One day as I sat upon a sunlit rock
I heard the sound of horses' hooves going clippety-clop
Diving swiftly below into the safety of the sea
I furtively broke surface to see the captain staring at me

"Lass, I know you are from the sea
Nevertheless I would like you to accompany me
Through the woodlands on horseback I will take you
We'll cross over the moors in the early morning dew

"I will show you hundreds of flowers in the lea
And you can tell me of your life in the sea
Together we will share what is in our hearts
A strong bond we'll build for the times we are apart"

He would sit on the hillside resting on one arm
Twirling a blade of grass between his lips, only adding to his charm
Something drew together these two souls of the sea
Slowly unfolding into what was forever to be

A bond so strong it endured even death
For the sea enveloped Lorelei into its breadth
A storm raging through my heart and my soul
Drowning, sinking, into depths far below

I will sound out the feelings I have long submerged
The past and the present I must now converge
As I cast off this dark shadow of grief
From where I sit upon this reef

For something still flickers like a moonlit night at sea
A whisper on the breeze heard only by me
A sail before the wind, a force I cannot see
A knowing in my heart forever there is he

Part V – *Uncharted Waters*

Facts surrounding the existence of mermaids are as fluid as the sea itself. Until they become crystal clear, wading through the murkiness of uncharted waters will help us draw our own conclusions.

Do You Know Me?

I am from the sea
Do you know me?

Perhaps you think of me as legend or folklore
Stories made up by those who came before
A tale spun throughout the ages
Passed between generations in varying stages
A myth stretching farther than the expanse of the sea
The very reason you no longer recognize me

Do you know me?
I am like you and you are like me
The only difference is that I live in the sea

The qualities that make you what you are
Also exist in me
Uniquely human, uniquely mermaid
The only difference is the sea

About The Author

Aerwyna is the author and webmaster of UniquelyMermaid.com, a website devoted to the beauty and poetry of mermaids, with unique gifts, art, decor, and accessories.

Made in the USA
Monee, IL
10 December 2019